Another Way Home

*Stories of Encounters with God
On a Non-Religious Path toward Home*

Philip Scott

Another Way Home Publishing
Bolingbrook, Illinois

ISBN-13: 978-0615603438 (Another Way Home)

ISBN-10: 0615603432

Current photo of author on back of cover courtesy of
Leah Simonek Photography www.simonekphotography.com.

Front cover image purchased from Shutterstock.com

Foreword

I remember the very first time Phil asked me to read one of his short stories. As I read "Jesus Drove a '56 Ford" I was captured by the unique imagery he painted of a different kind of Jesus...one born of real live flesh and blood that changed the life of an unsuspecting little boy forever. From that moment on, I was hooked, eagerly anticipating the next story that Phil would deliver into my hands.

God has given Phil a special gift for bringing readers into a face to face encounter with God's love and truth through stories that come from a deep place in his own heart and walk with God. I believe that as you read these stories, you will be able to identify with the characters and ultimately discover a God who is closer than you think.

It has been my joy and privilege to travel "the path toward home" alongside this wonderful father, husband, friend and servant. I encourage you to grab a cup of your favorite beverage, find a quiet place, sit back and allow the Holy Spirit to speak to you.

Ken Hansen,
Lead Pastor
Living Water Community Church

Divine Co-Conspirators

Anything truly good that I have written in this book issued out of the power and life of God within me; I did nothing to merit it, but simply respond to the desire for the unequaled joy and happiness found in going where He leads.

It should come as no surprise that the One who "has Genesis 1:1 on His resume"[1] creatively uses all things, including people, to work together for my good and His glory. To that end, there have been countless and perhaps unwitting co-conspirators who've helped this writer escape the bondage of the kingdom of darkness. There are too many to mention them all, but here are a few:

The love, support, and godly dedication of my parents, Joe and Dee Scott, reminded me in some dark times of where The Light could be found. Though often uncertain of where it would lead me, they encouraged this searcher for Truth.

---

[1] This characterization I heard from Mike Bickle has often regrounded the sometimes disorienting arguments I have with myself about God.

The rich deposit of musical talent and love in my sister Meladee's heart continually nurtures my creativity.

The unswerving, patient love of my wife Joyce, even as my feet of clay sometimes track mud across our lives, encourages and challenges me to get up one more time, look past the façade of the safe, average life and dream.

The willingness of my kids, Erin, Jason, Kellen and Leah to risk and question the status quo has urged me to continue leaning into the process of thinking outside the box of comfortable ideas - to consider a different path. Your rich input of ideas from popular culture and visual arts helped me find a better way to articulate this book.

The loving support and honesty of Jim, Ronna, and David Grimes saved my life. The long talks as God led us one step at a time to see and take a better way home still inspire me. You are my best friends!

And thank you to...

Dr. John Piper for introducing me to the idea that hotly pursuing the unequaled joy and happiness found in God was not only an acceptable thing to do, but is in fact my life's greatest calling

Ken Gire for helping open the windows of my soul

John Eldridge - it really *is* a sacred romance

Jeff Imbach for leading me to the River within

Ken and Chrystal Hansen, and T.J. Harris, the most real pastors I know, for seeing the real me and standing with the impostor when he has been at his worst.

Matt Bauer for his friendship, valuable assistance with the cover and insights into publishing - you are talented beyond your years and a tangible example of God's presence with us in dark, confusing times.

Ellen and Brian Rasmussen for help editing this little book and just being reliable, honest friends.

Finally, thank you Caribou Coffee for really good coffee, a comfortable chair and a seemingly unlikely place to meet the King of the Universe.

Contents

My song is love
Love to the loveless shown
And it goes on
You don't have to be alone
Your heavy heart
Is made of stone
And it's so hard to see you clearly
You don't have to be on your own
You don't have to be on your own

And I'm not gonna take it back
And I'm not gonna say, "I don't mean that"
You're the target that I'm aiming at
Got to get that message home

My song is love
My song is love, unknown
But I'm on fire for you, clearly
You don't have to be alone
You don't have to be on your own

Lyrics by Coldplay from
"A Message"

Preface

"No matter where you go I will find you, if it takes a long, long time."

Lyrics by Ciaran Brennan from
"I Will Find You"

Home...

Hopefully, the word evokes feelings of security, warmth...the freedom to just let down and *be*. I understand that for many this unfortunately is not the case. But even for those whose homes were and are places to be avoided, I think the idea of home, a place of embracing refuge and peace, still beckons in unguarded moments from hardened, forgotten depths. I think this because I believe we're all born on unique paths, as it were, trying to *find* home. Everything we do is a veiled expression of this inexorable, deep longing, encompassing even the paradoxical, tragic expressions common in the human experience. As G.K. Chesterton observed,

> Every man who knocks on the door of a brothel is looking for God.

From the moment of our conception, we frantically claw at whatever will help us survive the inevitable heart-crushing traumas of infliction and denial. Unregenerated by the staggering Love that awaits us at our true home, we fearfully run to one mirage after another seeking relief.

It's all we know to do.

In the process, we are intentionally and unintentionally shoved further and further from our real home at the hands of a diseased world filled with diseased people like us. As it was with Neo in *The Matrix*, the eyes of our heart are blinded to reality by the *Cosmos Diabolicus* in which we are immersed.

In our search for home we travel unique paths bounded and paved by family, friends, ethnic and national origins, and life experiences. But as different as our paths and the reasons we're on them may be they have this in common:

> The path we're on is not the path God wanted us to choose.

Though it sounds discouraging, think about it for just a moment. As exciting, blissful, and confident as life may seem at the moment, even if we're awash in His tangible presence, He would rather that we had never left home at all. God's desire is that we had stayed home, that we had not succumbed to fear, taken our inheritance and squandered it far from home[2] on that which can never satisfy our deepest need to be abundantly thriving in and powerfully manifesting the nourishing presence of Real Love.

The good news is that, motivated by pure love, He continues to leave the ninety-nine[3] to find us wandering dead-end paths of self-righteousness, empty religion, humanistic philosophies, all manner of addictions, materialism, and apathy. The lyrics to the once popular country music song by the same name capture this ubiquitous human tendency:

> "Looking for love in all the wrong places,
> looking for love in too many faces,
> searching your eyes, looking for traces of
> what I'm dreaming of..."

But His limitless creative genius uniquely meets each of us where we are. He entices us home refusing to conform to preconceived notions about what He is and isn't, soveriegnly choosing to open our eyes with whatever

---

[2] Luke 15.11-13
[3] Luke 15:4

mud[4] He deems to be most effective for the moment. When we see that which we have never seen before, we need to tell others – we *need* to tell this part of our story. Bethany Dillon and Ed Cash framed this truth in the following lyrics from *Dreamer*.

> "Love came and whispered a story and awakened a dream."

The stories in this book issued out of my encounters with God. They are the mud God has used at significant moments in my life, many written long after the events they describe. I believe He did this to open the eyes of my heart and sharpen my understanding of Him and the reality hidden deep beneath the temporal surface of these moments.

Notably, God didn't remind me of them in settings commonly thought of as sacred. Instead of church services, religious conferences, prayer meetings, or Bible studies, God often chose the blatantly nonreligious setting of a coffee shop and memories to help me see my way toward home. I believe He did this, not because the religious settings are invalid, but for reasons that likely have to do with my inability to hear Him without

---

[4] John 9:6

instinctively superimposing my learned religious filters. I explain more about this in the *Introduction*, but as Ray LaMontagne so simply expressed in the song "Old Before My Time."

> It took so long to see that Truth was all around me.

As you read these stories, open up, and let God invade your life in ways that don't conform to customary constructs. It can be a bit unsettling, but as C.S. Lewis aptly stated,

> God is not a tame God, He is wild, but He is good.

At the end of each story, there are blank pages for journal notes, so get yourself a hot beverage and settle in with your heart open to God.

Ahead on whatever path you're on, He runs for you, arms open, wildly spinning[5], tears of joy running down to a wide grin. Hear the song He sings over you, and embrace his complete, perfect love and forgiveness.[6]

---

[5] Dennis Jernigan's life-changing characterization of Zephaniah 3 :17
[6] Zephaniah 3:17

Father, give us eyes to see and ears to hear "... how near is your Kingdom!"[7]

---

[7] Dale Wisely, the Undisputed King of Internet Whistle Journalism

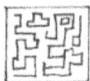

Introduction

In the *Preface*, I alluded to learned religious filters that I believe have negatively impacted my ability to accept perceiving God in nontraditional ways. In this section, I provide a context for this belief.

Writing of this sort necessarily involves one's family of origin and the religious bent, if any, of one's parents. Clarity is crucial so let me begin by stating that were it not for the hardworking, supportive, God-loving character of my parents I would have had a much harder life. As it was, they steadfastly provided life's necessities, a few luxuries, and consistently pointed me and my sister toward God.

However, in the process of helping parent four of the finest people on the planet, I have learned that all parents, especially me, are often unintentionally imperfect, which is to say that we're unaware of the negative impact of some of the influences of our parenting. The consequences may not surface for many years, if they surface at all, but it is quite unavoidable. Let me start at the beginning.

I was raised in the Southern Baptist denomination of Protestantism. We attended Sunday school and worship services on Sunday morning and again on Sunday evening. Yearly revivals, Vacation Bible School, youth programs and summer camps, mid week covered dish dinners and prayer meetings were regular events. Life at the local church was a major part of my formative years.

The idea of God and my relationship to Him was formed and hardened in the air of this consistent exposure. Much like an MTV video that indelibly burns images destined to forever be summoned when one hears the music, it was unavoidably imparted to me that the God I was learning about was defined by and in the religious practices and spiritual disciplines of my local church. Not only did my church *tell* me about God, as they understood Him, it was the conduit *through* which flowed my experience *of* Him.

As a young boy, my idea of Jesus was framed in the flannel graph, maturing later into the white-robed sage with glowing face consistently portrayed in "Christian" movies. Scholarly exegesis ingrained a reflexive understanding of scripture and doctrine that left little room for variant approaches or alternate interpretations. Even teachers who recognized the essential role of the Spirit in functionally gleaning the deepest meanings of scripture seemed to expect that the Spirit would choose to solely exercise His role within the boundaries of denominationally acceptable hermeneutics. Watching television at home, attending school, or playing outside was not discouraged, but these activities were secular, and therefore not to be considered the spiritual equal of what happened at the church.

The idea that the Spirit would use these everyday activities and experiences to communicate crucial insights into His character and nature was seldom, if ever, mentioned from the pulpit or in any Sunday school teaching. The latter was likely due to the fact that many teachers simply delivered the materials published in the teachers' manuals that were prepared by denominationally approved experts.

I came to see that I gradually assimilated this same "Christian" mindset. Even though I secretly had questions about what I was being taught, when one believes questioning one's teachers is tantamount to questioning God himself, the choice to ignore the questions is an easy one. I just copied what I saw and understood to be prized by the church leadership. As the spokesmen for God, if they were pleased, then I reasoned so was God.

In my early 20's, the inner struggle reached a head when I decided to no longer deny the desire for an amorphous "something else" that festered within me. Even though in some substantial way I thought I might be disappointing God, I decided to stop denying myself, and to no longer "take up my cross and follow Him." At that time I understood that anything I enjoyed was to be denied and that to identify with Christ meant choosing suffering over happiness. An acceptable way to demonstrate a proper love of God was to become a missionary in a place deemed the most inhospitably forsaken. Church camp bonfires solemnly invited us to throw in our lighted sticks thereby symbolizing our resolve to destroy our implicitly selfish, secular ambitions and suffer with Christ.

There in the flickering darkness tearful prayers were whispered to God promising to become missionaries to Africa.

Inwardly, though, I saw myself as a hopeless case who was just too secular for God. Nevertheless, I did what was necessary to maintain an acceptably religious exterior.

As you will read about in the stories *God Will Be God* and again in *You Will Be My Witness* some personally devastating events revealed the emptiness in my theological house of cards. The reconstruction on these razed ruins took me down paths that weren't theologically acceptable in my denomination. What's more, I soon discovered that I became just as limited in my view of God on these new paths. I am often reminded that where the Infinite Other Than is concerned, incomplete understanding is an ever-present companion.

Again, in no way do I mean to suggest that experiencing God is not possible in overtly religious or denominational settings. Rather, I offer the following stories as a testament to the idea that the abundant life promised by Jesus runs within us like a river and that river meanders throughout the infinite reaches of life.

The Night God Gave Me the Finger

I didn't come to condemn you, but to save you.

- John 3:17

Sometime during the mid-to-late '90's, my wife and I attended a three-day conference on prayer. I wasn't overly excited at the prospect of hearing others speak on a subject that, truth be told, seemed either too structured and clichéd, or too mysterious and impractical.

What more did I need to learn?

At some point during the conference, I opted to attend one of the break-out seminars by myself, while the others in our group went to different ones. The seminar facilitator instructed me to simply ask God a question, then quiet myself, listen, and write down what came to me.

I smiled as I considered asking God if I could have several more questions, but a single, serious question immediately asserted itself, pushing its way to the front of the line:

Why do I feel the need to be right?

I was all too aware of the fact that as far back as I could remember, I hated being wrong. Being wrong wasn't simply a momentary disappointment; it inexplicably carried with it the weight of life and death.

I needed to be certain that what I believed to be factual wasn't just my opinion - that what I believed to be the truth *was* the truth. Of course, knowing that what one believes *is* the truth isn't often, if ever, an easy proposition. In this world, shades of gray often contend with the easy comfort of black and white answers and muddy the waters of clearer streams of consciousness.

But amid the swirling, shaken snow globe of opinion there was at least one glaring, irrefutable reality smirking in the corner. I was absolutely certain that I often was *not* sure I was right. I knew it and my family and friends knew it.

The blood of this undeniable reality was in the water and to survive, I quickly developed the verbal skills needed to make a convincing case for what I *wanted* to be right. If I wasn't sure I was right, I would argue to make it right, ironically keeping the truth at bay. I hated being this way.

Why did being right matter so much?

God's answer came in the memory of a recurring nightmare that I experienced during a two-year hospitalization.

I was only four when an affliction known as Legg-Perthes left my parents no other practical choice but to check me into Children's Hospital in Baltimore. The nurses reported that I sobbed uncontrollably for two days, and then suddenly seemed to come to terms with my new home.

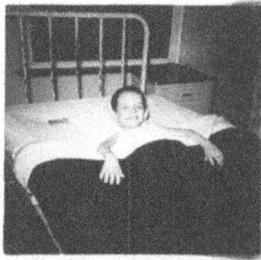

What they didn't know was that to my four-year-old mind, I was left in this place because there was something fundamentally wrong with me - not just a physical infirmity, but a flaw in the deeper, core essence of who I was. Feeling abandoned there in the hospital ward and with all the internal strength I could muster I made a vow to never be wrong again.

The subconscious energy in this inner struggle for survival and restoration found its way into my dreams the significance of which was about to be revealed now some forty-five years later in the memory that follows.

T he darkness came in a clicking wave as the night nurse turned off each row of lights. There was no escape. Securely fastened to the mattress with elastic straps across my Perthes-ravaged legs, thin waist, and shallow chest the darkness soon covered me and I wondered if "they" would come for me tonight.

Soon I would be asleep, but dreaming that I was still awake - waiting, full of fear that they would come. Lying motionless, I starved my lungs on short, shallow breaths as I stared intently at the wall at the end of the ward, waiting for the first sign of their arrival.

Then I saw it. The wall slowly changed from its usual faded, off-white to a gray hue barely distinguishable in the shadowy darkness. Soon though, it darkened to a malevolent black swirl that opened a portal. It was time to close my eyes and, with all the convincing strength I possessed, pretend to be asleep. Almost immediately after the portal opening solidified, they emerged. A troop of malformed, gnome-like creatures poured from the portal like ants from a disturbed hill and began checking each boy in each bed to see if they were awake. Working their way from the far end of the ward, they would soon be at my bedside. Even though my eyes were tightly shut, I could sense their approach as the air around my bed seemed to grow heavy and moisten with their foul stench. I squeezed my eyes shut in hopes it would still my trembling frame.

In a single moment, all the scurrying stopped. I knew one of them – the leader I assumed – was staring right at my face waiting and watching for a telltale sign of disobedient wakefulness. In the lingering quiet of the moment, I could hear the barely audible rasp of their labored breathing. Maybe this time they would be satisfied and leave me alone.

But just when hope began rising, I felt the bed move. The creaking frame and squeaking wheels heralded to the rest of the troop that one had been found awake.

They began wheeling me toward the portal, gleefully clucking and giggling with their prize. I remained motionless, thinking maybe it would give them pause to reconsider. But as they turned my bed toward the yawning portal, I knew my fate was sealed. They wheeled me through the opening into a dark, foreboding place where nothing good could happen.

My bed stopped just inside the portal. As I heard my captors leave my bedside, I slowly opened my eyes to the dimly lit interior. A few yards away, the squat, grotesque gnomes frantically milled about, frequently eyeing me to make sure I was still on the bed as they busily prepared whatever excruciating punishment they would soon inflict on me.

I had tried so hard to comply – to be asleep like all the other boys. But, as always, I failed. Now, quaking in the dread of what lay ahead, I suddenly sat upright and swung my legs over the edge of my bed, looking for all the world like I was going to make a run for it. I couldn't remember what it was like to run. I wondered if I would collapse in a tangle of atrophied legs when my feet hit the floor.

Instantly, the room grew quiet as the gnomes stopped their work and turned to face me with blank faces and blinkless stares. I could feel the energy level in the room building as they seemed to sense I was about to bolt.

Then it happened.

Just as I could almost see them leaning en masse toward me, I raised my right hand, arm outstretched toward the ceiling, as if wanting to ask or answer a question. But instead of waving my arm, I curled my hand into a fist and shot my index finger skyward.

Immediately, the crowd of captors began looking at one another, their mouths gaped open in stark amazement. Then several of them rushed over to my bed. I recoiled thinking this was it.

But instead of attacking me, they began wildly tearing at the sheets and blankets, as if searching for something. The others scattered around the room, screeching and chattering in a cacophony of panic and fear. They, too, seemed to be looking for something as they opened drawers and cabinets and pulled furniture away from the walls. Their change in focus diminished the hopeless dread in the pit of my stomach, replaced by an oddly timed sense of curiosity.

What was going on?

Soon my arm, growing heavy, lowered and I relaxed my fist. As if a switch has been thrown, the bulbous heads of the panicked little creatures swung in unison to stare right at me. Now it was my mouth that gaped in a bewildered stupor.

What had just happened!?

As the gnomes' faces glowed with contorted glee, the sick knot of fear returned and I began to weep. Now they would finish what they had started.

No sooner had I slumped in resignation to my fate than once again my right arm shot straight up and I pointed to the sky. Right on cue, the gnomes scrambled once again, driven mad by some unknown, invisible force. And then it struck me: Invisible! The gnomes were looking for me! For some reason, when I pointed upward, I was invisible to them. They couldn't hurt me because they couldn't find me.

As a flood of sweet relief washed through me, I quickly lowered my arm just for the pleasure of watching their faces switch from glee to confusion when I raised it again.

In the midst of this triumphant sense of joy, I woke up.

After reliving the dream, many pieces seemed to fall into place. I knew God was telling me that He didn't care if I got it right or not, He loved me and would not let my enemies take me. All I had to do was let him lead me to the one way home... the one way from where I was to where He was. The one way...wait a minute! One way!

As if to validate what had just happened in the auditorium at the conference, God reminded me about the iconic symbol that accompanied the Jesus People movement of the '60's.

But instead of an intolerant, argumentative symbol justifying my condemnation of the beliefs of others, it became a sign post pointing the way home.

As the crushing weight of the need to be right lifted, there in the lightness of just being with the Lover of my soul, I smiled as I realized that God had prophetically given me this symbol of His rescuing love in a nightmare *ten years* before He gave to the Jesus People to share with the world.

Notes

Jesus Drove a '56 Ford

I will be with you always, even when the world ends.

- Matthew 28:20

I hadn't been sitting long on the concrete step that marked the front door of our Cape Cod claim on a piece of mid-fifties suburbia. It was always the first stop, the place where my six-year-old imagination waited for inspiration. As I was about to pursue a fantasy loosely based on a creek and the endless possibilities it offered, I heard the unmistakable, throaty rumble of the modified exhaust, accompanied by the crunching scratch of rubber on gravel as he rounded the corner.

Norman was home.

His gray '56 Ford Customline coasted neatly to a squeakless stop in front of his house next door. I knew I had time, as I always did, to get back inside where the safety of home would be between me and him; where the manliness of my Dad with newspaper and coffee was more than a match for Norman's D.A.[8] and taut, tattooed biceps.

But I froze, as I always did, indecisively snagged between raw fear and a compelling curiosity.   Maybe it was that relaxed, confident stride, tinged with just a hint of arrogant purpose, the taps on his plain black boots scuffing the pavement like the suburban version of jingling spurs. Maybe it was the way he took one last draw on the stubby cigarette that hung precariously from his lips just before he deftly flicked it in a slow, arching statement that screamed of indifference to custom and tradition.   No doubt about it: Norman was cool and his coolness was petrifying. I couldn't move and perhaps this is what would save me.   If I sat there as motionless as a lawn jockey, breathing only when the mammalian instinct insisted, he might just miss me altogether. The alternative was simply too fraught with uncertainty to consider.

I was only six, with pipe cleaner arms and legs.   I was released from Children's Hospital in Baltimore the winter before after two years of flat-on-my-back bondage to Legg-Perthes.   Now the fast, able-bodied boys in my first grade

---

[8] The D.A., short for Duck's Ass, became an emblematic coiffure of disaffected young males across the English-speaking world during the 1950s.

class took occasional joy in knocking me to the ground for the encore pleasure of watching me try to get back up encumbered by crutches, a braced leg and big-soled shoe.

The coolness of Norman coexisting with such white-hot incapacity was simply not possible within any known system of interpersonal dynamics. If he saw me, The Theory of Impeccable Coolness, demanding that equilibrium be restored, would render me so completely trivial I just might cease to exist altogether.

I don't know. Maybe his piercing eyes caught a subtle shudder. Perhaps he just smelled the fear. Whatever gave me away, Norman abruptly veered and headed straight for me like a predator on scent. His eyes locked onto mine, as his pace quickened like that of a lion about to break into a full, deadly run after some easy, infirm prey. He was on me in an instant. I had waited too long to go inside. He stopped, silhouetted by the morning sun like a dark monolithic tower, and spoke.

"Hey, kid. What's your name?"

I was so utterly unprepared for this prelude to annihilation that I could only muster a feeble "huh?" in response.

"I'm Norman," he said gently, as he offered his hand.

I stared in disbelief at his immense, rock-knuckled hand looming before me, palm slightly upturned and inviting. Too afraid to resist, I placed my small, trembling hand in this iron vice that could crush it to a fine powder. There was no turning back now.

But the startling lightness of his touch, masking the callused power in his grip, felt strangely safe like the reassuring hold of one who wouldn't let me plunge to my death. Norman slowly pumped my arm, and smiled.

"Does that thing hurt?" he quizzed, motioning toward my brace.

"Uh... no," I ventured with eyes quickly averting.

"You must be pretty strong to be able to walk with that on your leg," he said as he lowered himself to sit next to me.

I didn't know what to say. I could only stare, bewildered, at the new grass greening in the warm spring air. Strong? *Me?*

As if he heard my thoughts, he said, "Yeah I know lots of kids who wouldn't be able to walk with a thing like that on 'em."

"Oh, it ain't hard," I ventured.
Pressed now to balance Norman's unexpected praise with what would doubtless be a demand that I perform I quickly added, "I can't run too good though."

"Yeah, I bet," he agreed, "but one day you will."

The confident certainty of his words kindled an ember of hope.

"You've got lots of time to get better. Just keep trying and playing hard," he advised. "I'll help you whenever you need it," he affirmed.

I found myself turning now to look fully at Norman. His face seemed soft, almost gentle. He smiled and playfully rubbed my close-cut hair.

"Well, I gotta go. Uh, whaddya say your name is?" he quizzed as he rose to leave.

"Philip," I quickly answered. A blush of regret surged as I feared my name would seem dumb to him. As the fear swelled, I scrambled again for the quick comfort of lowering my head.

"You know what, Philip?" he asked, lips cocked in an approving smile and eyes glistening with pleasure. "You're a pretty cool kid. See ya 'round."

I watched as Norman strode off to his front door. He turned and smiled, waving just as he disappeared into his house. I worked my way to my feet, and stood there transfixed by the tantalizing air of a feeling so foreign, yet so sweet in its fragrant wake. I was oblivious to time as a warm wave of quiet energy washed through me. Things within, twisted and jumbled for so long, were being placed in a settling order.

"I have to go to the store," a voice interrupted.

I turned, slowly coming back to the reality of the here and now, to see my dad standing on the other side of the screen door.

"If you want me to, I'll carry you to the car," he offered. I paused considering my options. Although I could walk, sometimes it was just easier for us both if he carried me.

"No," I firmly replied, "I wanna walk. Come on Dad, *I'll race ya!*

Notes

Brahma Bull Woods

A window into God's Invitation to risk

An unfamiliar paradigm for how God speaks began emerging several years ago with the reading of Ken Gire's widely acclaimed work *Windows of the Soul.* With simple clarity he penned a gently persuasive case for the surprising ways that God speaks to us – ways that we'll miss if we insist on limiting our hearing of His voice to what can often be the sterile confines of academic Bible study.

To be sure, connecting with God through less well-defined sources messes with the comfort of predictability, but as Ken wrote, if we close this window we'll likely miss the singing of the birds and the warmth of the sun. For me, it has been particularly intriguing as I see God using some of my childhood experiences to model the things He is teaching me as an adult. Brahma Bull Woods is just such an experience.

Perhaps this is one dimension of His insightful declaration in Matthew 18:3 that becoming as little children is a prerequisite to seeing the Kingdom of God.

The reds, yellows and golds of mid-autumn fluttered brightly against a crisp, blue sky. October's chill cooled my skin that otherwise warmed in the brilliant sunlight of half a morning gone. I stood staring at the dirt path that narrowed as it entered and then disappeared into the verdant, shadowy world of Brahma Bull Woods. It was a good day to die.

Brahma Bull Woods lay on the edge of the neighborhood playground, a juxtaposition of polar opposites if ever there was one. Just a few yards from the frolicking carefree world of swing sets, sliding boards and jungle gym sprawled a land of petrifying uncertainty. I often played near the creek that babbled invitingly at the entrance, but always with one eye on the woods. I had heard the stories the older boys told about Tommy Carter; how he'd gone in and down the path a bit too far; how no one had missed him until after the street lights were on and everyone was heading home to warm suppers; how the search party of reassuring deputies and pipe-smoking fathers in their car coats had eventually found his gored, lifeless body tossed into the underbrush like a candy wrapper. The story had the expected impact. I stayed out of the woods.

No one actually came right out and said it. The keepers of the story preferred to let imaginations do their dirty work. The name "Brahma Bull Woods" planted the seed, and the fact that a horned bovine of some description wandered the fenced field next to the woods watered the rich soil of a child's mind too young to question what his eyes could plainly see. Though no one actually saw it happen, that bull had run Tommy clear through.

I suppose it was the woods' reputation as a place of death that established its traversing as the rite of passage it now was. All I knew was only two things could fend off would-be bullies: having recently been released from reform school, or traversing Brahma Bull Woods alone. The former was like a social wild card, and could be played to demonstrate superior knowledge about fighting, law, and the world at large. It obviated the need to traverse the woods at all. For the masses though, the path to acceptance and acknowledged bravery went straight through the woods.

As the youngest kid in the larger circle of rabble that ran the streets of the west side, opportunity had come knocking. Though I hovered somewhere near the bottom of the pecking order, surviving a trip through the woods could catapult me right over all of the eight year-olds, and most of the nine year-olds. I'd be on the doorstep of the double–digit crowd; the rarified air of those who routinely played outside past dark, said "damn" with impunity, and spit with astonishing regularity.

So here I stood on destiny's doorstep. I had been here many times before, but had been backed down by a festering fear in the pit of my stomach. But this day there was no turning back because just days before, on the heels of a round of mindless name calling, I had forced a premature end to the exchange by announcing that I would be "doing the woods" on Saturday. The funeral-like hush that fell over the gathering crowd left no doubt that everyone had heard the boast. I immediately turned and walked away, knees threatening to buckle beneath the leaden regret. Whispers of disbelief punctuated by the requisite "Aww, he'll chicken out!" proclaimed by some unwashed cynic, battered my hastening retreat like a handful of stinging pebbles.

All week I hoped the parental factor would kick in and force me to go somewhere, anywhere else. But Saturday morning found my mom doing laundry, my dad preparing to mow the grass, and my friends trolling the street in front of my house like morbid spectators watching a gallows being constructed in the town square. I dressed slowly, giving every chance to some intervening authority to open a back door, but a stoic resignation soon swallowed that desperate illusion: there would be no last-minute reprieves today.

The only question that remained was whether to wear shoes or go barefooted. A good pair of sneakers offered protection from splinters, rocks, and the random broken whiskey bottle, but the extra speed afforded by running barefooted was a well-established fact. In the end, I opened the front door and stepped out to face my fate wearing shoes and the grim face of one who knew he was in way over his buzz-cut head.

Now at the edge of the woods, the senior eleven year-old spat, and spoke. He may as well have been God himself.

"Okay, Philly-boy, here's the deal. You gotta go all the way through the woods, to the highway, through the pipe, and back again. I'll know if you did 'cause there's somethin' on the other side of the pipe. When you get back, *if* you get back, tell me what you saw and I'll know you made the trip. Got it?"

I nodded with decided ambivalence, my mouth as dry as bones bleaching in the desert sun. An inciting shove got me weakly moving toward the path.

The wind swelled as I entered the woods, as if closing a door on the world I had known, and muffling the voices and laughter of the onlookers behind me.

I stopped to survey the path and the woods. Shadows, twists, turns - how far was the end? How long was the pipe? *Where was the bull?* For a brief second I wondered if I could just double-back through a different part of the woods, go home and forget the whole thing. But somewhere down in the unexplored regions of my being I understood I couldn't settle for less than the promise of what lay on the other side of the trip through this fire. Some things are worse than death.

As I timidly passed the first stand of tall trees, from the brilliant, sun-lit land of the familiar into strange, deep shadows, I paused to take in the moment. The well-worn path took a sharp right turn and disappeared through a wall of underbrush. My heart pounded rhythmically accompanied by short, shallow breaths. I stepped forward, forcing myself to place one foot in front of the other until I had turned the corner through the bushes.

This first challenge met, I was presented with a new section of path. It was straight and level for about fifty feet, and then... well, it simply vanished. A blank, blinking stare attended my all-out attempt to find some rational mooring for what I saw. *Did the path end there? How would I know which way to go if there wasn't a path? No one said there wouldn't be a path! Then again, no one said there would be one either.* The internal debate soon threatened to commandeer the mental energy I intuitively knew I needed for other battles.

In a recklessly bold moment, I burst into a full run, covering the short distance to the where the path seemed to end. I stopped abruptly and dropped in a low crouch, inwardly chastising my impulsiveness and praying the bull hadn't seen me. I discovered to my tenuous relief that the path actually continued in a steep, winding, descent to the creek. The rules that would govern my decision-making began to take shape. As long as there was a path I would keep going.

I kept to that rule, winding my way through the woods at a slow trot, and stopping periodically to scan the forest for any sign of the bull. Satisfied he wasn't around, as I resumed my trek, I walked slowly at first then broke into the trot as confidence pushed the fear to a corner of my consciousness. I actually began entertaining the idea that perhaps the bull was napping on a belly full of field grass when I heard a totally unfamiliar noise that seemed to ride somewhere between the windy whoosh of the treetops and the gurgle of the creek. Fear uncurled, and stood to its feet, moving toward my fragile confidence like a grinning thug.

I edged my way to a nearby tree, hoping I could hide my frailness from whatever was making this unearthly sound. I looked for movement everywhere, sucking air in a frantic gasp when a couple of startled birds fluttered out of the dense thatch behind me. Seeing an opening, Reason presented a simple, three-word plan to address the current crisis: run home *now*! I turned slowly to begin my flailing sprint for life, but, as I turned, movement off behind some distant trees caught my eye. I looked back, and wait! There it was again... and *again*! Each time as I saw an image crossing from left to right, I heard that odd noise. I instantly understood what I was seeing and, more to the point, what I was hearing: these were cars on the highway. The highway was just ahead!

Within minutes, my careful trot brought me to the base of the steep hill on which the highway rested. The path simply dissolved into the creek. A small finger of the creek entered a galvanized culvert that cut through the hill to the other side of the highway. This must be the pipe. I paused to take in the significance of the moment: I was only fifty yards from half-way to glory.

Bending only slightly, I peered cautiously into the pipe. A small stream of water glistened in its dim, corrugated interior. At the far end, the pipe's exit blazed like a beckoning beacon, full of promise and reward. I stooped and stepped in.

Straddling the streamlet, my fingertips touching the pipe's ribbed circumference to steady my waddle-like progression, I moved steadily past small rocks, accumulated debris, and through spider webs that stuck to my sweaty face like gluey nets. I simply pawed them off my eyes and lips and kept moving, too focused now to consider whether or not their owners were home when I uprooted them. It wasn't long before I was at the far end.

As I stepped out of the pipe and straightened up, a cool breeze washed over me, reminding me that it was autumn. The intermittent whining whoosh of the passing cars above complained that I had conquered the highway. Smiling confidently, I began studying the unfolding scene. What was I supposed to see?

At first glance, I didn't see anything worthy of such enticing mystery. Color-laden trees swayed, tall grass, groomed by the wind, nodded uniformly. A seemingly motionless, shallow pool of water gathered just below the pipe's edge. Coiling my thin leg muscles, I leapt over the small pool to a large rock worn flat by years of exposure to the relentless pounding of wind and water. It was from this new vantage point on the rock that I saw what had to be the closely guarded secret of the woods.

Just behind some sentinel maples, stretched the remains of a tree house. I picked my way through the tangle of undergrowth to get a closer look. Only a few gray, rotting floorboards and a failing ladder of loose slats had survived. Just as I lifted my leg to test the strength of the lowest slat, the air was split by an unholy sound so gutturally primeval that I screamed, jumped, spun around, and back peddled in a one continuous motion like a startled cat. Unlike a cat, though, l landed in a heap under the cross members. It all happened so quickly, the full realization that it must be the bull only now exploded into my consciousness, sending waves of horror rippling through my frail frame.

Panting with a heaving hoarseness, I vainly tried to crab backwards on all fours... then slowed my panicked scramble... then stopped.   The bull was nowhere in sight. With a sudden twist, I flipped over and looked behind me, then rolled over quickly and sat straight up again. No bull. My eyes darted left and then right. No bull.   What had made that horrifying sound?

As if cued by some invisible director, the driver of an eighteen-wheeler up on the highway, for reason's known only to him, decided that very moment to employ the rig's Jake-brake, sending a resonant, ear-splitting snort belching from the exhaust stack.

From my seated position, I closed my eyes and fell straight back on the forgiving fall carpet.   Relief coursed through my body, as the adrenaline high subsided with each breath. With a deep sigh that signaled the official end of this latest scare, I slowly rose to my feet.   Standing, I noticed a raft of deep scars that festooned one of the trees. Hearts with initials, words I didn't recognize, and a simple declarative sentence that completed the day's journey: There is no bull.

I read the sentence silently at first, then again, forming the words with my lips: There is no bull. The third time I said them aloud. "There is no bull!" then a fourth time, slowly savoring each word's contribution to a burgeoning joy. "There... is... no... bull!"

The once terrifying cloud that shrouded the woods evaporated to resolve the simple, but challenging neighborhood myth.   I raced back to the neighborhood, fueled by a transcendent connection to conquerors of evil empires and their own compromise of comfort.

Exiting the woods, I slowed to a purposeful strut, as some of my friends, pointing excitedly, ran to greet me. A warm satisfaction settled in companionable silence, teasing out a broad smile. It was a great day to live!

———

In 1995, my wife and I visited my old neighborhood. The streets seemed narrower, but the familiar surroundings evoked easily relived moments, stringing them together like the pearls they are.

The woods, though, disappointed me. Somehow they seemed shallow and unimpressive. How could I have been so terrified?

In reflecting on this, I realized that Brahma Bull Woods had different names for me now, names like

"What if I don't succeed?"
"What if I have cancer?"
"What if I'm never happy again?"
"What if this is as good as it gets?"

These new woods are a lifetime deep, and I've been told the "bull" is toothless and tired. But the only way to know for certain, the only way to experience the Truth, is to go through them.

As surely as He was with me on that October day in 1957, He has been with me everyday since. He opened this window that I might remember how it felt, like Jesus, to risk it all for the joy of what lay beyond[9] what I could see and know - that I might have the courage to simply take the next step.

---

[9] Hebrews 12:2

Notes

The Blessing Beyond
the Boredom

God's purposes revealed in the commonplace

Much of our lives, we act out of patterns and rhythms
socialized into our psyches from birth. Along the way, the
message that "life is hard and then you die" sneaks past
our despairing search for something more. We gradually
lose the sense of intentionality and slip into living life by
rote - working, worshipping, and sleeping our way to
mediocrity. A deep sigh reveals our resignation to hang on
until Jesus takes us home.

But there may be more to the commonplace than our
hearts, yearning for the excitement of the journey, can
appreciate when buried by kids, cars, and mortgage
payments. There are sudden events that spin our heads
around in their uniqueness like a splash of red on a
background of gray scale. In an instant God reveals a rich
purpose in what be appeared to have been the ignoble,
even counterproductive hum-drum of life on planet earth
leading up to that event.

In 1972, as a crewmember of the aircraft carrier U.S.S. Midway, I experienced just such a moment one night in the Gulf of Tonkin, forty miles off the coast of the then war-torn country of Vietnam. This is the story.

"Tell Scott to get up to Radar 2 ASAP! We gotta wounded bird inbound!" The blaring voice from the intercom jolted me out of my letter-writing reverie, and I was already un-dogging the heavy door of the maintenance shop as my supervisor responded. Darting quietly through darkened berthing compartments and down vacant passageways traveled dozens of times before, I knew every hatch, every knee knocker, and every ladder, so my mind started wondering what series of events had led to this moment. The sheer energy in the call told me there was no time for explanations, and as promised in boot camp, I had been trained to react without question. Boot camp... it was there that I first found myself wondering just what momentary insanity had led me to enlist in the Navy. There were times when I understood in my bones why "N-A-V-Y" truly meant Never Again Volunteer Yourself.

My uncle, who was also a sailor, had imparted wisdom when he counseled me that the way to survive Navy boot camp could be summed up in two concise axioms: shut up, and do what you're told.

As I would later discover, keeping these two rules wouldn't make boot camp a pleasant experience, but it would mitigate the pain as the keepers of military tradition once more began the process of dismantling the civilian way of interacting with reality. Eighty long-haired boys with overblown egos and accustomed to sleeping way too much were about to embark on a ten-week journey of self-discovery designed by professionals, and honed to near perfection over centuries of application. I figured I would follow the two rules, keep a low profile, and do my time.

I was wrong.

Sometime after arriving at the Recruit Training Command, San Diego, after the stylish haircut, uniform issue, medical and dental probes, and aptitude testing, the company commander of Company 077 got in my face and informed me that, in his absence, I had the responsibility of making sure the company learned to march, and arrive at all the required classes on time. It seems the fact that I had been in the Air Force ROTC program at Baylor University for all of one semester now entitled me to feel all of the blood in my head rush to my feet and a knot of nausea the size of the battleship New Jersey form in my stomach. Without thinking, I forced myself to incant the boot camp mantra:

"Sir, yes sir!"

But even though there were many sleepless nights for two weeks after that unnerving event, something deeper than the fear of failure compelled me to meet this challenge. That something deeper was the fear of not having tried. At several times in my life to this point I had backed down when confronted by the possibility of failure at the next level of growth in sports, music, and college. Once again, I was being presented with a chance to step up and accept an intimidating challenge for which I knew I was totally unprepared.

Ten exhausting, but maturing weeks later, I graduated with honors, and could sharply maneuver those eighty young men through a variety of impressive close order drills.

This same process of "challenge-fear-acceptance" would be repeated many times over the course of my six-year enlistment. After boot camp, I was sent to a variety of Navy schools to study electronics, radar, and tactical data systems. When I explained to the Navy that the only thing electronic I understood was that when one turns the volume knob on the car radio clockwise, the sound gets louder, I was told "That's why we're sending you to school."

Sixteen months later, I was ordered to the aircraft carrier U.S.S. Midway to support the repair and maintenance of, among other systems, a powerful radio that transmitted remote control landing data to aircraft. In the event the pilot was unable to land the aircraft on the flight deck, this system would... at least that was the claim.

Soon after reporting aboard, the ship was ordered back to the Gulf of Tonkin to provide air support for the war in Vietnam. There was much to learn about living and staying alive on a 65,000 ton ship loaded with tens of thousands of pounds of ordnance, but I soon found that as big as the ship was, after a year or so, it became small, the work became routine, even boring, and I wondered whether all this training, schooling, and time was worth the cost and trouble. At sea for 75-80 days at a time, one day became just like the next. The only events that drew hopeful interest were the possibility of mail from home, or a supply of fresh milk. I faithfully maintained the systems assigned to me, not knowing if it really even mattered.

You see, I had never witnessed the aircraft landing system perform its feat of remote control magic. Even though each year during refresher training and carrier qualifications the pilots were supposed to take their hands off the stick and allow the system to land the aircraft, I was told off the record by many of them that the last thing they would ever do is let something else take control of their aircraft. They would just make sure they were getting the data and call it "good."

I arrived now at Radar 2, a small compartment in the island structure, and saw that the radio system was predictably ready to perform its designed intent just like it was every day since I first stroked its gray steel cabinet and said "Hi sweetheart! We're gonna be friends!"

What I didn't know was that minutes before I arrived in Radar 2, 1000 watts of Ultra High Frequency power had sped data to an A6 Intruder All Weather Attack Jet some 15 miles away. The aircraft was in serious trouble as the result of a 20mm anti-aircraft round entering the cockpit, fatally wounding the co-pilot and seriously wounding the pilot. Just before passing out, the pilot flipped on the Automatic Carrier Landing System switch.

Minutes later, the aircraft caught the #2 arresting wire and safely came to a stop on the deck.

The pilot was saved.

When these details were recounted to me later, every day before and every day after took on a strengthening new meaning. As I reflected on the cost of it all, I understood what is best explained by a contemporary ad campaign:

- My pay, training, food, and uniforms...thousands of dollars
- The system that landed the aircraft...hundreds of thousands of dollars
- The aircraft...millions of dollars
- The pilot's life...priceless

Tolstoy is credited with having said that boredom is the desire for desire. When we decide to engage our destiny, the journey won't always be an exciting adventure. Most days the biggest challenge will be to once again do the simple things we know to do even though the exact reason has faded to a dim memory.

When life seems to be about as appealing as digging a hole, remember you are unearthing a treasure of great price one shovel-full at a time, and, although one scoop of rocky dirt looks pretty much the same as the previous one, each one is uniquely closer to the destiny.

Notes

Between the Shoulders of the Father

Even the hairs on your head are numbered

- Luke 12:7

Erin's deep brown eyes began the nightly slide toward sleep as I placed her in the warm, soapy bath water. Though precocious beyond her three years, she was totally unaware of what I could see all too clearly as she spoke to me of bubbles, fish, and her busy day: Erin would be asleep before I could get her dried and dressed and into her bed.

After a few minutes of play, I cupped water over her short cut hair that still seemed to glisten with the day's sun. I smiled as she bravely closed her eyes so tightly that her nose wrinkled, and held her breath in anticipation of the waterfall that would cascade down her face. She loved to show me that she was a big girl. I wondered if she knew how her every movement, even the subtlest nuance of her personality, captivated me in silent wonder.

A bit of shampoo and soon her hair was a mound of whipped cream, a peaked soft serve cone, or a candle flame. She knew the list of make believe, and fought sleep until we had achieved each one for her to gleefully inspect in a small mirror.

But as I rinsed her hair beneath the tub faucet, the talk and laughter subsided as the energy in her small frame twirled with the bathwater down the gurgling drain. Slippery and sleepy, I wrapped her in a thick towel and sat her now limp little body on my lap. With her head lying against my chest, I swayed, letting the thirsty terry cloth do its work. For several minutes I gently rocked her, coaxing her approaching dreams with homemade tunes hummed just above a whisper. Moving with slow deliberation, I ran the large wide comb through her drying hair, stopping to remove the few strands that accumulated from time to time.

It was there... in this memory... that I met God again for the first time.

As I watched each counted strand float into the wastebasket, the ancient words penned by the good-news writer Luke suddenly transfixed my consciousness with the beckoning promise of life: "... even the hairs of your head are numbered..."

Years of Bible study, polluted by a stoic, performance-based religion, had cast a sterile, empirical light on my God in white-lab coat, clipboard in hand. His knowledge of the number of hairs on my head just came with being omniscient.

But in this moment of eternity, the soiled, whitewash of that clinical tombstone gave way beneath the life-giving weight of His words:

> "Your love for her is but a shadow of my love for you."

The Creator of the Universe had stepped out of the pages of my worn Bible, out from behind the cloud of mystery to find me again at the moment and in the place of my greatest need. Masterfully weaving together the words of his heart, given to a first century physician, with the twentieth century memory of my love for my daughter, God once again invited me to fall against his chest and rest in the assurance of His never-ending delight and joy in me. While the "love of God" had been reduced to a theological construct in my life, He came now, not scolding me for my folly, but by becoming who He needed to be for me in that place and time – by becoming *me* embracing my daughter after her bath.

In this moment of eternity, He took the shortest path to my broken, wounded heart and continued to beckon the emerging life.

Immersed in His presence, I once again knew what it meant to live... and move... and have my being.[10]

---

[10] Acts 17:28

Notes

God Will Be God

No one knows the thoughts of God except the Spirit of God.

- 1 Corinthians 2: 11

At the very heart of orthodox Christian faith is the belief that God is supremely sovereign; that He alone decides what He will and will not do, and singularly possesses all knowledge and power to execute whatever is His good pleasure. While I completely agree, I have encountered irreconcilable views as this profound tenet has been unpacked - views that left me wrestling with conflicting notions of what I really believe about His sovereignty. As the subtitle says, this is an unfolding revelation. In no way do I believe I have now arrived at the complete answer.

I've heard it said that we Christians make a huge mistake when we "... take to conclusion that which God has only revealed in part." I only want to share what I have learned so far, offering it for your prayerful scrutiny and consideration.

I was raised in a denominational tradition that imparted the notion that as long as what I wanted lined up with Scripture, God was obligated to perform in predictable ways. This seemed especially true if I could check-off the corresponding boxes on the weekly offering envelope, attesting to having daily read my Bible, attended worship services, tithed, and studied my Sunday School lesson. Armed with His own Word and in the face of such documented commitment, I believed God's favorable response to my wants was virtually assured.

Not surprisingly, when my first wife filed for divorce in 1988, I sped to Malachi 2:16 where God clearly states that He "... hates divorce" then to the myriad passages in the Psalms detailing the deliverance of the righteous by an angry God, confidently concluding that He would not allow this terrible thing to befall me and my innocent children. I read books about restored marriages, and listened to hours of testimonial tapes about miraculous reconciliations. Fully armed with scripture, energizing faith, and blossoming hope, I rejected all discouraging thoughts that seeped in... except one.

I was in a counseling group at the time and, as the ripping and tearing of the divorce-machine continued unabated, I sought the counselor's assurance that God would indeed intervene and rescue me and my kids. What the counselor said, as I hopefully listened for confirmation, was "All I can say is God will be God." Disappointingly, no supporting definitions of exactly *how* He would be God were offered.

In that moment, my neatly constructed cause and effect paradigm began to crack like cheap pottery. I was deeply troubled by the prospect that, while I could withstand having *my* expectations of God sorely disappointed, the fragile, uninformed faith of my children would surely be crushed, propelling them into a rebellious hatred and mistrust of God. I was too blinded by pain and anger to understand that God's love for me, my children, and, most notably, my departing wife was infinitely more pure and caring than mine. At least part of my motivation for wanting God to stop the divorce was not wanting to face the consequences of my contributions to the breakup of our family. While I gave lip service to accepting part of the blame, I continued loudly pointing to the fact that *she* was the one filing for divorce!

Sometime later I heard Larry Crabb speak about the inborn mistrust we all have of God's goodness. Gradually, God revealed that the reason I attached expectations to His goodness, by inwardly demanding that He rescue me from painful situations, was that I didn't trust Him to know what was best for me in the context of my *deepest* needs. Like an art critic with his nose only six inches from an infinitely huge painting, what I could see was woefully limited. With this revelation, my focus began to dramatically shift.

I stopped focusing on what my wife was doing, and began seeing and hating the rottenness in *me*. Healing tears of remorse poured as God gently brought me face-to-face with my sin, and then strongly embraced me in the reality of His unwavering love for me. Though I had no savings, a broken car, and had just lost my job, the energizing, undisectable peace and joy imparted by His loving presence removed all expectation that He deliver me. The external problems lost their intimidating, preoccupying power.

There was a time on this journey when, if someone else had written these things, I would have inwardly anticipated that the next paragraph would detail how God, honoring a new found attitude, restored the marriage, the job, and all that was lost. One only has to read Job to know that God *does* do that. But I have found that, whether He does or doesn't, He is being God. In my case, the divorce was final in 1993 and my former wife remarried a year or so later. But I am convinced that part of God being God is that even when the very thing we so desperately hope to avoid falls squarely upon us, He is uniquely capable of using it for our good and His glory. As we place our trust in Him to be who He is, we find He has already prepared a way for us to become, not simply survivors, but rejoicing conquerors.

Are there specific things we can expect of God without being presumptuous? Yes, I believe we can expect Him to love us with a love that compelled Him to die rather than live without us; a love that permits us to experience whatever it takes to bring us to a place of ever-increasing trust in His goodness; a love that won't allow us to settle for the shallow illusion of a wrinkle-free life.

I'm not sure I can guarantee anything else, but beyond the assurance that He loves me with a love that intentionally works all things for my good, I'm not sure I really need anything else.

Notes

You Will Be My Witness

The life-changing power of sharing your story

There are times when the most innocent intrusion – a cardinal on a tree branch, a golden leaf twisting in the breeze, a shaft of dusty sunlight - seizes control of my usual task-oriented approach to the day, and transports me to another place and time. Early on a fall morning in 1992, I drifted back to northeastern Wyoming. Still employed as an engineer with a major oil company, I was driving a rented Jeep down the virtually deserted lease roads, meandering back to an array of crude oil storage tanks that lay hidden behind the stark, rolling barrenness of mid-winter. I was careful to observe the local protocol when the rare pickup approached from the opposite direction. Only the most flagrantly uninformed would greet the oncoming driver with a full wave. Like work boots that looked and smelled of new leather, such a wave was a rookie giveaway. Veterans of the oil patch simply raised a forefinger off the steering wheel, a technique I practiced until I achieved the proper balance of politeness and nonchalance. Just as Devil's Tower was coming into view and the prong-horned antelope, running alongside like dolphins in wake of a ship's bow, looked as if they'd dart across the road in front of me, she knocked on the open door.

"Good morning, Phil. Do you have a minute?" I stared at Linda for an extra, preoccupied second, as my mind made the trip back to Chicagoland.

"Oh, hi...yeah, sorry....uh, sure, please come in!" I offered, trying to recover.

Linda and her husband Stan owned a corporate outplacement service where, due to a massive downsizing by that oil company, I found myself fine-tuning my resume, calling my network of professional contacts, and wondering how it would all turn out. Linda was here to welcome me officially.

She confidently strode over to the desk and offered her hand in the expected business-like manner. Everything about her was in order – hair, makeup, shoes, and crisp business suit. Her every movement was flawlessly choreographed with the polished air of a practiced business professional.

"Stan and I like to personally welcome each of our clients," she opened. "I want to let you know that we understand this is a stressful time for you and that we'll do our best to help you get the kind of employment you need...to help you get whole again. Do you have a minute to talk?" she inquired.

"Sure. I was just daydreaming," I explained.

"Well it's good to get away once in a while, isn't it?" she said, with a knowing smile.

We spent the next five minutes briefly discussing my work experience, career ambitions, professional plans, and expectations. I stuck to the script such exchanges require, not revealing that the loss of my job was just the latest in a hail of life's arrows that had found their mark squarely in the heart of my best-laid plans. This most recent arrow found company with the emotional carnage surrounding the unwanted divorce my wife had been energetically pursuing for the past two years, and the wanton disregard my car demonstrated for my fragile state by demanding a new clutch.

Quickly, though, the official veneer began to dull as Linda paused for a moment, then got up and closed the door. A reflexive concern, ingrained by hours of corporate sexual harassment training, was quickly alleviated by the fact that two large glass windows bordered the door.

"Phil, may I ask you something personal?" she almost pleaded.

"Well... yeah, I guess" I replied.

"I hope I'm not prying, but since the day you started coming here, I've noticed that there's something about you – the way you seem to approach this situation," she explained.

My mind began parsing her words. Situation? Approach? Something about *me*? Perhaps she was mistaking me for someone else.

"I mean, you and Mike both seem confident and peaceful, while so many of our clients seem genuinely afraid of the future. What's your secret?" she asked directly.

Mike was another job-seeker I had met early in my job hunt. I noticed him one day, and, as he looked at me, I saw a kindred light in his eyes. He smiled and introduced himself, and asked, right there at the front desk in a foyer full of strangers, "You've met Jesus, haven't you?" That encounter started a brief, lunchtime relationship of mutual support and the occasional hallway prayer for God's hand in our lives.

Still unsure of what Linda was looking for, I considered about how best to tell her my story. I thoughtfully fingered a pen and, looking out the window, began recounting how in 1988 I had two, dramatic encounters with God:

He showed up the first time as I was trying to orchestrate my own happiness apart from what I deeply knew was His will. My failing attempts at creative rationalization and the resulting anger, as I realized there was no way out, left me face down in a black, inky depression. I lived a low function, fetal life, disconnected emotionally from every familiar support. The faces of my children waxed into the lifeless visages of department store mannequins. I was in deep weeds.

The second encounter came when the unrelenting pain had convinced me to end it all. As I was struggling to remember where I had put the firing pin to my rifle, a guttural groan barely escaped my lips, "Oh,

*Gaahhhhhhd... help me." I slumped in surrender,
unable to form even the most primitive expectation.*

*Imperceptibly, like words whispered in a wind, a wave
of warmth began flowing through my body. It started
at the top of my head and, in a crescendo, oozed down
like a healing balm until it puddled at my feet. The
consuming, gut-wrenching despair vanished so utterly
and completely that I wondered if it had all just been a
nightmarishly real dream. Intense joy and an infusion
of a love I had never known before caused me to laugh
out loud. In a place so much deeper than the surface
dogma of empirical considerations, I knew it was Him.*

There was a muffled sniffle and I realized I hadn't looked at
Linda even once while telling my story. I turned now to
see her gently weeping, mascara blackened tears lining her
face, and her nose openly running.

"Linda! Are you okay? I'm really sorry if I upset..."

"Oh, no, please. You don't understand," she quickly
interrupted. She went on to explain how she had been
raised in the church, but found the whole God thing so
implausible and the Christian life a joyless, judgmental
bore. But she confessed that the life she and Stan lived

now, though supported by all the materialistic rewards for their entrepreneurial determination, left her constantly trying to fill the ever-present, pain-ridden vacuum with still more stuff.

Linda explained, "Phil, what you don't know is that just this morning, in desperation *I* cried out to God. I said 'If you're real, please send me someone who knows you!"

The sharp, unflappable demeanor of this got-it-all-together professional was replaced now by a soft, engaging gentleness. With genuine, penetrating eye contact, she tearfully thanked me, smiled, and excused herself to go clean up.

As I thought about what had just happened, an inner voice spoke.

"You will be my witness."

Witnessing.

I couldn't help remembering the time I had spent going door-to-door, as part of the evangelistic outreach of the church of my youth. With tracts in hand, teams of us descended on the front doors of unsuspecting neighborhood residents.

While just moments before answering our knock, they may have been watching their favorite TV program, napping, or engaged in other just-living-life pursuits, they were now confronted with a question, recently arrived from left-field, posed by total strangers:

> "If you died tonight, do you know whether
> or not you would go to heaven?"

The required change in focus was tantamount to suddenly throwing a speeding car into reverse. I could see the vapid bewilderment in their faces as they tried to switch gears from the everyday to the eternal. Another witnessing strategy was to befriend a coworker or neighbor with the ultimate objective of "winning them to Christ." Everyday conversations, veiling the greater agenda of a trek down Romans' Road, reeked of that pseudo sincerity common to fanatical, multi-level marketing devotees.

While each of these well-intentioned strategies may be a good tool, they are at best impotent in the hands of those who have no direct, life-changing experience informing their assertions. The life-giving Word becomes little more than a legal brief, a source document to support an argument. I participated because my local church placed value on such activities. I reasoned that the leadership would see me as mature if I showed up, and if the leadership approved of me, God approved of me.

It never occurred to me that, since I could not speak out of a first-hand experience of the deep, transforming change I professed, God had no expectation that I would bear witness to it. I came to understand years later that He was actually pleased with me just the way I was and, more to the point, was delighted to direct my experiential understanding of Him and of completing, in perfectly timed, incremental steps, the good work He had begun in me.

I don't know what became of Linda and Stan. My term at the outplacement office ended shortly after the encounter. But I started learning, on that morning back in 1992, that as I intentionally pursue the Lover of my Soul, He will lead me into an unfolding revelation of Himself and my true identity. I won't have to *try* to be like Jesus. When the same Spirit that empowered Him to do and say what the Father showed Him operates freely in my heart, I *will* be His witness.

Out of the Life that is in me, the supernatural reclamation of the lost will overflow the confining walls of programmed soul-winning and into the day-to-day reality of genuine relationships.

Notes

One Last Thing

It seems to me that uniqueness within unity is crucial to a healthy Body - that we not try to become carbon copies of one another, and find ourselves stifled and unwilling to risk authentically becoming the unique embodiment of boundless Love that God made us to be. In her times alone with God, Sarah Young, author of *Jesus Calling*, felt God telling her,

> "I am leading you along a way that is uniquely right for you. The closer to Me you grow, the more fully you become your true self – the one I designed you to be."

I believe she heard from God. "Church", as it is practiced in many settings, paradoxically provides, amidst the programs and orders of service, an easy place to hide from God and one another. We can simply follow the crowd into an acceptable ritualized sameness. While this is arguably not the goal of the leadership in most local expressions of the Body of Christ, it is almost unavoidable if one does not intentionally cultivate and nurture a rich, personal experience of God in the larger context of one's life.

In *Beautiful Outlaw: Experiencing the Playful, Disruptive, Extravagant Personality of Jesus* author John Eldredge makes the following point:

> Now here is a tough pill to swallow. In the Gospel of Matthew Jesus has thirty-four intimate encounters with an individual—"intimate" defined as when someone in particular is singled out for mention, or receives a word or touch from Jesus, or Jesus receives a word or touch from them. Of the thirty-four, one takes place in church. In the shorter Gospel of Mark, there are twenty-six such encounters recorded; two take place at church.
>
> Furthermore, all of the most "famous" stories about Jesus—his birth, baptism, trial in the desert, calling of his disciples, turning water into wine, raising the dead, transfiguration, walking on water, feeding of the five thousand, Sermon on the mount, calming the storm, Last Supper, dark night in Gethsemane, crucifixion and
> Resurrection - not one of them takes place in church. Not one. This is no coincidence. Jesus came to the most religious people on earth, and much of what he had to do in order to bring them to God was to free them from their religion.

John goes on to assert that in those days if one wanted an intimate encounter with Jesus, one would have been "... far more likely to find it outside church." Given that we spend on average about two hours in church each week, it seems likely that this should still be true. But are we open to it or have we subconsciously allowed "church" to almost exclusively define and mediate the presence of God in our lives?

While I fervently hope that you enjoyed the stories, my greater desire is that, apart from the time you spend at the local church, they helped unearth a fresh well of God's life-giving presence in your life. I hope they created in you an expectation of Jesus everywhere, anytime, and made you hungrily open to His speaking to you in infinitely creative ways and places.

No matter where you are on your path toward home listen for that still small voice and rest in the confidence that the One who chose to die rather than live without you knows where you are and *He will find you*.

I invite your comments at www.anotherwayhome.net

Phil Scott